Parenting

for
Technology Futures

Part 1: Education & Technology

Illah Reza Nourbakhsh

ISBN-10: 1505880432
ISBN-13: 978-1505880434

To Nikou, Mitra and Marti

CONTENTS

ACKNOWLEDGMENTS

As technology evolves ever more rapidly, the concept of technology fluency becomes only more relevant to all our decisions. The definitions and motivations underlying my understanding of technology fluency were borne of interactions between the Carnegie Mellon University CREATE Lab and UPCLOSE at the Learning Research and Development Center of the University of Pittsburgh. I am grateful to the staff of both institutions for helping me realize that the key to taming our technology future is to empower families to concentrate, more than ever, on authentic human interaction.

My reviewers' comments have been invaluable to evolving the ideas and presentation of this book. Professor Fatemeh Zarghami, Early Childhood and Human Development instructor at De Anza College, and Professor Junlei Li, Psychological Science and Early Learning & Children's Media researcher at St. Vincent College and the Fred Rogers Center, provided comprehensive comments on drafts of this text. They played a pivotal role in guiding my thinking about the developmental process of parent-child interaction that matters most, and in helping me understand how to best communicate with my audience. Thanks also to Junlei Li for his expert identification of relevant quotes from the writings of Fred Rogers, who showed so much wisdom throughout his life about the relationship we strive to develop with our children. Carolyn Noorbakhsh and Marti Louw provided guidance during the formative writing stage, encouraging me to complete what I started so we can share as broadly as possible.

Note: my blog, **robotfutures.org**, will track news stories and on-line discussions relevant to PARENTING FOR TECHNOLOGY FUTURES.

1 INTRODUCTION

In *Robot Futures* I argued that technology's role in society is rapidly evolving, and that the new relationship between robotic technologies, corporations and citizens can have dystopian consequences on our freedom of choice and our sense of identity. But society also faces a new and serious structural danger: ever-increasing chronic underemployment as the boundary of robot capability consistently marches forward, overtaking human job categories with less expensive, more corporation-friendly machine alternatives. But although these technologically powered trends are global and long term, most readers who contact me are most concerned with one key ramification—uncertainty about their children's future:

> *How do I give my child the best possible preparation for a post-human future powered by technology?*

The standard answer is to be a good parent by making sure your child fulfills her potential to be a creative, socially facile, passionate, loving and confident person. After all, these are timeless character traits that enable a child to adapt to all the unknowable changes that the future will bring.

But in a time of severe technological change, these essential character traits are not the whole story. If we want our children to flourish in a technology-rich future, we need them to understand

1

technology deeply— so deeply that our kids influence the future of technology rather than simply being techno-consumers, along for the ride. In short, we wish to prepare our children so well that they influence the robot future. We call this level of future mastery *technology fluency*.

In education today there is frequent public discourse on *technology literacy*. After all, as electronics pervades our lives, we all must learn how to use computing systems thoroughly. But the standard of technology literacy is far too modest. It sentences us to be users of products, with our sights set on the goal of correctly employing electronic products and digital media without hesitation. We become consumers of the technology future, addicted to apps in the cloud just like a goldfish depends on a power above to rain down daily fish flakes.

Fluency is about inverting this consumer-facing power relationship between technology and humanity. When we are technologically fluent, we are creative producers rather than robotic consumers. We understand the limits and possibilities embedded in machines and computers, and we know how to change the way technology functions and thereby change its impact on society. We become innovators, capable of inventing an appropriate technology future rather than being caught in the currents driving us towards an undesirable one. As robotic technologies pervade society, I believe the best chance we have for our children's success is to ensure that they are socially aware prophets of technology innovation rather than nearsighted consumers of technology.

With this book, my goal is to provide parents with the background knowledge and strategies to help their children achieve this form of technology fluency. These writings are organized into two releases: Part 1 on education issues and Part 2 on recipes for fluency. *Part 1: Education & Technology* provides background tutorials on education and technology trends that are essential to navigating home and school learning today. With the tutorials under your belt, you will be primed to make informed choices concerning existing educational tech trends. You will be ready to have fruitful conversations with your child's teachers and principal on parent-teacher meeting days.

The tutorials are each standalone and informational. Feel free to read them in any order. Next year I plan to release *Part 2: Tech Fluency Recipes*. This second publication will describe friendly building blocks for technology fluency, suggesting activities and resources that will help nurture your child's fluency, one skill at a time, across the developmental range. The skills are arranged in cumulative order, with each subsequent skill building upon the strengths your child will gain through earlier experiences.

Education & Technology Tutorials

Parents face a major challenge as new technology education trends wash through the educational system: how does one separate the hype of new trends from the reality of true educational change? What are the most important ways a parent can support learning in light of new trends—by engaging with teachers and after-school programs, and by providing the right space and tools at home?

One major national policy debate concerns the educational skills called *STEM*: science, technology, engineering and math. Policymakers and schools have embraced the idea that the U.S. has a massive deficit of STEM training for future scientists, engineers and technologists, and this awareness has led to reformulated school curricula which emphasize STEM classes, often at the expense of other disciplines that emphasize communication and creativity. Chapter 2, *STEM Education*, explains both sides of the STEM policy debate and provides guidelines for how to evaluate and influence the STEM strategy in your school.

Another major category of debate is on the Education Policy side. As in many countries, we in the U.S. are forever berating the educational system as being inferior to many of our peer countries in the developing world. New efforts consistently attempt to provide a national fix: No Child Left Behind and Race To the Top are two White House programs that became political landmines with real consequences on how public schools function on a day-to-day basis.

The one truism is that there are no quick fixes to our educational system, and so you can justifiably view any bearer of a quick fix with immediate suspicion. Chapter 3, *Standards, Testing and Accountability*, provides you with an overview of how government programs have changed the way students and teachers are evaluated and rewarded for progress. This will prepare you for examining how testing and accountability are affecting the quality of your child's education in your specific school, and this in turn sets you up with the knowledge to advocate for the right type of change.

Chapter 3, *Digital Learning*, introduces new learning technologies that are transforming on-line education. Some schools have attempted to reinvent the entire educational experience as a giant computer game in an attempt to make learning as fun as video game-playing. *Gamification*, as this technique is called, is popular in business as well as education, and it is important to understand how the reality of gamification sizes up to its promise. Another highly individualized learning technology, the cognitive tutor, is designed to provide one-on-one computer attention to students, adjusting to just the right rate for each individual student. Yet the results of educational studies using cognitive tutor software are mixed, demonstrating that the social in-class experience still proves to be the major influence on true learning.

Finally, the classroom is being augmented both by teachers and by parents using on-line interactives such as Massive On-line Open Curricula, or *MOOC's*. Some even argued until recently that MOOC's and on-line learning will replace universities and schools altogether. While the excitement over on-line learning has diminished somewhat, parents are consistently seeing their children come home with assignments that include both educational on-line games to play in the evening and on-line course lectures to watch, for instance on Khan Academy. In the Digital Learning chapter I describe gamification, cognitive tutors and on-line courses in detail, summarizing their advantages as well as important cautions.

These tutorials are meant to aid you in several ways: they will help prepare you to team up with parents, educators, administrators and school board members in fruitful ways, to understand how technology is treated at school, and to help you advocate for the best possible education strategies in the classroom. This information will also prepare you to interact more closely with your child regarding digital learning tools, so that you can better understand how she uses technology day-to-day in completing homework assignments and in further exploring and nurturing technological interests during out-of-school time.

Of course the chapters in this book are only starting points, and there is a great deal of excellent writing on these subjects on the Internet and in local libraries. Rather than provide footnote-based references throughout the chapters, I have appended each chapter with a *Reading Resources* endnote that describes a handful of articles and books that are especially informative. I have carefully selected the books and papers I believe are truly worth your time, so I do encourage you to tap into these resources.

Tech Fluency Recipes

Preparing yourself and your child for the best possible school experience is a powerful way to combat the poor use of technology, whether at a school-wide policy level or inside a single classroom. But school time is only 20% of your child's waking hours. The more important question is, how can out-of-school time best enable your child to become technologically fluent? Done well, the best out-of-school experiences will nurture a love of learning that will help a student make the most of school, and will also support the best possible life decisions in our rapidly changing world.

Technology fluency is a broad topic, and I believe strongly that for every individual the pathways to this form of personal empowerment are totally unique. Yet all paths share some common features. Your child must first develop a sense of wonder and curiosity in the early years (during preschool years) that drives the desire to learn, and must also learn how to learn—how to translate curiosity and

5

motivation into the mastery that will provide strong, satisfying internal rewards. Together, the motivation to learn and the ability to learn provide the twin guide rails for exploring the physical and technological worlds in sufficient depth to achieve deep fluency.

These are large and abstract goals, but I believe we can break down the enablers of technology fluency into six specific skills that reinforce one-another. *Part 2: Tech Fluency Recipes* will present six cumulative skills that I believe can blossom through out-of-school activities—six muscles that together activate into general technical fluency. Each chapter will define a specific skill, then introduce guidelines and resources for activities relating to the skill. You are the best judge of your child's abilities and interests, and so the activities are not strict recipes, but rather flexible options that you can tailor according to your family's tastes. Here is a sneak preview of the topics for each skill chapter:

Chapter 1 - Identification is built upon the recognition that the physical world and the built world are replete with diversity and complexity, and that recognizing similarities and differences in systematic ways helps us fundamentally understand how to think about patterns of information. From identifying mushrooms and macroinvertebrates to recognizing makes and models of cars, there are activities across the age range that build a child's eye for observation, pattern-finding and identification.

Chapter 2 - Feedback focuses on how the complexity of the world can be viewed in terms of interrelationships. In the study of engineering and computer science, feedback loops are critical to understanding any system that is responsive to its surroundings, from thermostats to automobiles. Natural systems, from ecosystems to the human body, depend equally on feedback loops that govern the essence of how biology functions. Numerous activities for a range of ages foster an intuition for complex systems and feedback, using the home, backyard, the weather, on-line simulations and other easily accessible resources as systems for exploration and experimentation.

Chapter 3 - Internalization suggests activities that help a child develop a personal agenda based on the ability to self-motivate and empathize. A loved child has an environment that is consistent and nurturing. Then high self-esteem flows from the realization that the consequences of her actions are predictable and fair. Self-esteem, in turn, encourages experimentation and active decision-making—critical skills for building up a personal sense of courage. With courage comes the willingness to risk, to fail and then to try again without feeling demoralized. This is the crucible of perseverance, which is a life skill for social problem-solving and for technological problem-solving as well. All of this starts with internalization and consistency, but the ramifications stretch far beyond these early ingredients. Chapter 3 is an action chapter, with project ideas that will help nurture the drive to have a personal, empowered role in an emotionally meaningful complex system. Examples that serve as both powerful motivators and important learning reinforcement include plant and animal care, volunteering with a local conservancy dedicated to ecological management and other personally driven home projects.

Chapter 4 - Diagnosis reflects on activities that empower the child to ask questions, make measurements, detect errors and make corrections. Many technologically successful individuals talk about taking apart everything at home when they were growing up. This is one such example of a sense of repair: the critical realization that everything can be understood when a strong sense of inquiry, the power of observation, and a confident sense of experimentation are combined. In this chapter I suggest both repair activities and other exploratory activities that strengthen these same mental muscles, turning every technology from a magical black box into a puzzle worth revealing, exploring and understanding.

Chapter 5 - Invention addresses a fast-growing and exciting aspect of robotics and creativity: the Maker movement. While many institutions support making, from children's museums and science museums to TechShops throughout the U.S., the activities that are critical to inspiring children to really begin inventing are easily accessible through a broad set of materials and cost points. In this chapter I suggest starting points for engendering a sense of goal-driven invention at home and with little financial investment.

Chapter 6 - Mindfulness covers the most advanced and personal skill that builds toward technology fluency. Mindfulness is about enrolling the skills of identification, feedback, internalization, diagnosis and invention toward the most subtle, complex and empowering target: one's own self. Mindfulness builds upon and reinforces all skills while enabling the child to really understand their own body as an intricate system that deserves care, attention and management. I describe readily available technologies and visualizations that aid in the process of self-reflection and self-evaluation, and also provide powerful experiences for generating a sense of technology fluency through personal exploration. It is important to recognize that self-reflection and self-evaluation do not simply crystallize from within. You develop and express these very personal skills by being guided and by interacting with knowledgeable adults in your life. Once again, the most important of personal skills depends on the ecosystem surrounding the child—and you are the very best partner in improving and nurturing that ecosystem.

I believe the exploration of these six skills will foster a passion for learning and discovery that grows ever deeper. The child that explores with intensity and curiosity will build a new relationship with the technology she uses and the technology she invents: machines will cease to be commercial products meant to be used in one standard manner. Instead, technology will represent raw material, a grammar of sensing, visualization and computation to be molded in service of creative exploration and expression. That is true technology fluency.

Now back to this book, Part 1. I hope that you, the reader-parent, find the tutorials below to be valuable orientations to technology issues in a world where strong, partisan rhetoric often outshines balanced, actionable information. You want what is best for your child, and while we struggle with day-to-day choices, we are caught in a rapidly flowing river of massive technological change that threatens to drown out everyday decisions. I believe in-depth information on STEM, standards and digital learning will help you be as strategic as possible, empowering all the adults in your child's life to make the decisions that authentically support the future she deserves.

2 STEM LEARNING

STEM: Science, Technology, Engineering and Math. As a parent you have seen STEM not only paraded in the popular press, but also referenced by your school's administrators and your child's teachers. These four terms have risen to the top of the education debate because of two fundamental forces at work in education and politics: our desire to rate U.S. education in global terms, and our attempts to predict the jobs future of the nation, ensuring that our children gain the 21st century skills that are essential for 21st century jobs.

Most arguments about 21st century skills start by expanding on T: technology development is accelerating, and it is changing our lives ever more dramatically. To flourish in this technology-rich future, workers must be able to invent in the rich space of devices, software and interaction technologies. As for engineering and math, they are the languages that every technologist needs. Technology, in turn, is changing how we do science, from cancer research and digital medicine to space exploration. Science, in the 21st century sense, is one important way to apply technology mastery and enable major discoveries about ourselves and our world. As technology's advance continues to speed up, the argument goes, STEM training becomes ever more essential to our children's future because, without STEM, they will be left in the dust by the few who have that essential future job skill.

As for international standing, the STEM argument is straightforward and depressing. The U.S. compares well in math and science standardized tests with global average scores, but when we reduce our comparison group to just the industrialized nations, we are consistently near the bottom—in some cases 42nd out of 46 countries. If the future is defined by technology innovation, then our extremely poor standing sets our children up for a disadvantage right out of the gate: how can we hope for success if we start from a position of inferiority?

To really understand the STEM movement, we can first recognize that there are two very different flavors of STEM that educators and politicians espouse, and the distinction runs deep. The **Silo STEM** approach suggests that each of these four disciplines is an essential and distinct skill that every student needs, just as wedging, centering and pulling are three distinct skills that every potter needs to master. This balkanized mentality suggests that testing each skill individually is completely valid—and so standardized, skill-specific tests become milestones for educational success. In fact some areas, such as Math and Science, are much easier to define than broader disciplines like Technology, and so Silo STEM ends up designing and deploying math and science-specific standardized tests, often as a stand-in for all of STEM.

There is an important alternative that breaks down the barriers of the Silo STEM approach: **Blended STEM** recognizes how it is the interplay between technology, science, engineering and math that yields real 21st century innovation. The computer science equivalent of this concept is called *computational thinking*, which suggests that knowing how to use a computer is good, but understanding how the power of computing can be used for problem-solving across disciplines—that is true power. In the case of STEM, the scientist or engineer is especially effective because they learn how to think laterally, bringing all their knowledge to bear on the challenges they wish to surmount. Of course, why stop at these four disciplines? What about English, Arts and History? We will discuss that below.

But first, it is important to appreciate the scale of political action around Silo STEM. Government spending on STEM education spans fifteen federal agencies, with about 200 distinct federal programs spending in excess of $3 billion annually. At a countrywide level, the government sees STEM education as core to the nation's global competitiveness. And at a personal level, government also sees direct economic benefits: students majoring in STEM fields in college earn, on average, $300,000 more over their lifetime than others. But that isn't the top earning category—health care professionals and managers earn even more than STEM majors.

Moreover that $300,000 lifetime value is distributed highly unfairly. The STEM Achievement Gap is a stubborn reality of current government spending. As math standardized test scores have increased throughout the country for 40 years, the persistent demographic gap by race has not narrowed appreciably. African-American students aren't scoring as well as white students twenty years ago, much less catching up with their counterpart's 2013 test scores. In 2005, African-American students scored 26 points lower on math tests than white students. This statistic, which holds just as true in 4th grade as 8th grade, demonstrates enduring inequity in the structure of education, from lack of resources and less qualified teachers to limited access to accelerated courses when our schools are compared by socio-economic region. How is this reflected in eventual wages? Minorities and women are 65% of the labor workforce across the U.S., but hold only 25% of STEM-related jobs. Sadly, STEM itself is not an equalizer. Even the gender wage gap is just as stubborn in STEM jobs as in all other job types.

Now for more bad news. For the first time in 50 years, the majority of U.S. public school students are living in poverty. Consider the weight of this statistic, hard though it is to imagine. The majority of students have basic economic considerations affecting every aspect of learning, and this will directly challenge school's ability to engender a true love of learning. Health, nutrition, environment—all these core issues highly leverage the tools teachers can provide in school, and when the most basic needs of our students are unmet, then technology fluency, gender equity and socio-economic justice fall out of reach. When we live in a society where this economic gap is growing, not shrinking, for the youngest generation, then we are living the nightmare of an ever-increasing long-term gap in our nation.

How can you work to counteract the achievement gap? One very important role you have, as parents, is in addressing stereotypes. An excellent study by Claude Steele gave rise to the concept of *stereotype threat:* when students were given challenging GRE questions, if they were told that the questions were measuring intelligence, the racial achievement gap was clearly demonstrated in scores. But when they were told that the questions were not diagnostic for intelligence, the achievement gap collapsed. Stereotypes matter greatly, even in the minds of those who are victimized by them. Just believing that you are part of a class who will underachieve is enough to threaten your very performance, and self-confidence and positive self image are powerful ways to combat this vicious cycle.

The debate that echoes around the political blogosphere is just how much emphasis there should be on STEM-specific education. One argument gathering steam recently is that there simply won't be enough STEM jobs to justify all the educational capital we are spending. Some studies show 40% of STEM majors selecting non-STEM occupations, and unemployment rates for STEM majors remain unacceptably high since the Great Recession. An occupation distribution study from 1979 to 2009 demonstrates this well. The fastest increasing occupations are personal care, food preparation, sales, technicians, professionals and management, which occupy the top and the bottom of the salary distribution. The fastest decreasing occupations are operations, fabrication, laborers, production, craft, repair and office & administrative support, thanks to automation: squarely in the middle of U.S. salaries.

What's more, automation is improving rapidly, forever reducing the actual numbers of job slots in manufacturing and engineering, and so classical STEM-driven, middle-America opportunities are disappearing faster. But the recession's hit on unemployment has been broad, affecting non-STEM majors just as much. And alternatively the diversity of jobs taken on by STEM-educated students could be viewed as good news, demonstrating that these skills are valuable across a wide variety of job types.

If STEM is to help our children have a bright future, it cannot be Silo STEM that generates classic production or operations jobs: narrow knowledge for a narrow job type, even technical, cannot succeed as future robot automation steadily replaces and unravels job categories. Blended STEM is powerful because it integrates disciplines together, making our children broadly skilled enough to innovate in an uncertain future.

The educational impact of focusing on STEM is counter-intuitive in another important way. Standardized test-focused classes can be markedly uninspiring for many students, taking their initial excitement about science or math and dashing it with repetitive, dry curricula designed to maximize test scores. What's worse, retention rates in STEM-related courses are extremely poor, from computer science to engineering. The 2012 Presidential Report on STEM summarizes this problem, suggesting that post-secondary STEM courses ought to be research driven, so that students use their skills to solve problems they truly care about. But such curricular change will not happen overnight. Given the political, test-driven climate we live in, letting your child be exposed for the first time to STEM knowledge in the classroom is a dangerous gamble. They will be uninspired, and this first impression is a major lost opportunity.

In conclusion there is nothing truly special about the four specific disciplines of STEM. We need to accept that for all disciplines the blended approach is what truly improves learning. Whereas isolated STEM knowledge will not necessarily save a job from replacement by automation, the inspiration to bring knowledge from multiple disciplines together to solve any problem confidently will always have value. STEM has already morphed in many circles into STEAM – this is a healthy move because it incorporates Arts back into the family of core learning sensibilities, where it belongs. When your school talks of STEM, find out if they understand the dangers of balkanized, Silo STEM. Are they concentrating on each discipline independently for the sake of high test scores, or do they plan cross-discipline activities that tie science, computing and engineering together with arts? Have they heard of STEAM, and are they willing to be inclusive of all subjects rather than excluding English and history and art, which are so important to communication and expression, critical in our socially hyper-connected culture.

Most importantly, even as you work to ensure that your school crosses disciplinary boundaries and stops focusing on test results, you cannot depend on school as a first introduction to the joy of learning and discovery. By engaging with your child in science, art and engineering projects at home, you break down future stereotype threats and set up pathways for future success. Developing genuine interests early will also help your child overcome the uninspiring first class in a new subject, giving them the motivation to persevere until they can discover classwork that is truly exciting, rather than giving up early on an entire subject area and losing a future opportunity for engagement.

Silo STEM is a massive political movement now; it will steamroll into our future for years to come. Only by working the fringes at home and at school can we have real influence on just what form of STEM your child witnesses, and whether children can learn to connect learning across all disciplines.

STEM Reading Resources

STEM THE TIDE
This excellent 2011 book by David Drew quantifies the STEM gap between the U.S. educational system and the rest of the world, explains the achievement gap within the U.S., identifies success stories at both schools and colleges, and proposes how those successes could scale up to improve STEM education nationally.

ENGAGE TO EXCEL
This 2012 report by the President's Council of Advisors on Science and Technology advocates for one million additional STEM graduates. Although this goal is debatable, the report does an excellent job of summarizing how STEM education is implemented poorly today, leading to uninspired students and poor retention, and goes on to list specific techniques for reconfiguring STEM education altogether. The executive summary could be required reading for all parents, teachers and administrators.

SCIENCE, TECHNOLOGY, ENGINEERING, AND MATHEMATICS EDUCATION: A PRIMER
This 2012 Congressional Research Service report by Gonzalez and Kuenzi summarizes the politics and outcomes of STEM: how does the Federal government spend money on STEM, how has this translated into STEM degrees, and how do U.S. students compare to one-another and international peers across race and gender categories.

3 STANDARDS, TESTING AND ACCOUNTABILITY

School reform is the ultimate hot-button education issue. Everyone wants education to improve quickly, and several waves of reform have promised the one thing that is impossible in education: a quick fix. The real story of school reform is a tangled web of curricular standards, standardized tests and mechanisms for test-based accountability. We need to pick apart just what these trends mean, because the educational changes stemming from No Child Left Behind, Race to the Top, and our most recent Common Core and Next Generation Science Standards all have direct impact on how our students are exposed to technology, and whether school has any chance of nurturing technology fluency in our children.

Standards

Historically the power to set curricular standards has resided with each state. While this decentralization provides freedom for innovation across the country, it has also spurred ever-widening gaps between state standards, and therefore profound discrepancies between what children are expected to learn from one state to the next. But that is only one of many inconsistencies in how standards impact education. More fundamentally, standards that were once viewed as minimum requirements—a floor for what a student should learn at a particular grade level—are increasingly treated as the complete prescription for learning. The difference between these two interpretations is vast, and this rethinking of standards, from basic necessity to exhaustive plan, has several negative consequences.

When standards are basic and sparse, there is time in the schedule for teachers to go beyond the standards: to reach further based on their interests and current events; to innovate in the classroom, thus empowering their own profession and stimulating the students with customized experiences. In this model, everyone wins. But as standards proliferate, the attempt to meet every item and sub-item in a very long list becomes all-consuming for the teacher, and there is little time to be imaginative or responsive to classroom interest. The overly comprehensive standards become a complete recipe, and that leaves no intellectual or logistical space for variation and customization. As a result teachers become uniform and uniformly stressed; students receive more rote instruction in attempts to check every box. In this caricatured extreme, everyone loses.

Flexibility and freedom in the classroom can empower a teacher to be daring and exciting. More philosophically, standards that are comprehensive, rather than minimal, suggest that we ought to have the same educational goals for all students, and this is a subject of intense debate. After all, each individual student will have unique talents, and the space to nurture those talents must exist for every student to best unleash their potential. Normalizing the students would necessarily mean tamping down such differences, and this has risks hand in hand with the benefits of the average-case. So at the level of standards, the most important lesson is this: ensure that standards are treated as basic minimums for learning. They should not guide lesson plans, but rather they ought to be naturally met by every good teaching plan. Anything more, and standards begin to sap the enthusiasm out of teaching and learning.

As curricular debates at the state level over climate change and evolution have shown, even with the best of intentions state-level standards also become mired in politics rather than focused on serving the best interests of students. The recent national-level standards reform movements stem from this recognition that students across states witness significant inconsistency, all the more apparent as standards become curricula in unwholesome ways. The Common Core and Next Generation Science Standards (NGSS) are two such national standards movements. Because each state is autonomous in terms of standards, states must choose to ratify and use the Common Core and NGSS individually; so far forty-three states have adopted the Common Core. The debate about the value of these specific standards rages on and shows no signs of abating. On the positive side, the Common Core creates consistency across states, and this can be a good thing (subject to my caveats above) in terms of fairness and consistency.

However there are also detractions and weaknesses worth pointing out. First, the Common Core focuses on two specific subjects: Language Arts and Math. It does not provide real guidance regarding engineering, science, technology fluency, history, civics, music and art. Thus it is not an end-all solution to the problem of curricular standards, and this is important to understand because many states complain that they barely have the funding to create proper teacher training around Common Core, and therefore other standards, such as NGSS will simply have to wait years more. So the enthusiasm focused on Common Core, which covers only a narrow range of school subjects, can crowd out attention to other disciplines, making them accidental orphans.

Another potential Common Core weakness is that the standards are not equally great across ages or subjects. They stretch from Kindergarten through high school, and the most vociferous complaints appear to concentrate on the early childhood phase. No K-3 teachers participated in the early childhood standards creation, and three past presidents of the National Association for the Education of Young Children (NAEYC) have signed an open letter criticizing the Common Core for early childhood years.

Finally, there is the fact that national scale begets national marketing. Corporate interests—the same ones that have supplied shrink-wrapped curricula to schools for decades—are very excited by the prospect that national-scale standards create the opportunity to market new prepackaged material to every school in the U.S. Of course prepackaged curricula can raise the bar on the worst case; but it also squashes local innovation. You will want to find out how Common Core and standards, more generally, are treated by your school. Do school administrators explicitly design teaching to the standards, or do they use the standards as a check to ensure that locally designed curricula meets the standards and does much more than that? To what degree does the school use prepackaged, nationally distributed curricula, or rather do the teachers design their own curricula and lesson plans, with prepackaged materials viewed as tools in a toolbox to be sampled selectively and appropriately?

The Next Generation Science Standards represent the national-scale answer to the fact that the Common Core covers only math and language arts. Released in April 2013, NGSS is the newer, younger national movement that was designed by twenty-six states collaboratively and is, so far, adopted by fourteen states. NGSS covers physical, life and biological sciences most densely, with more moderate attention to engineering problem definitions and problem-solving approaches.

But even when state-sponsored, such a movement can run into political troubles, and this is demonstrated well by the case of Michigan, one of the states that participated in creating the NGSS. In September 2013, the Michigan House introduced a bill that, if enacted, will bar the state from using NGSS because it includes the phrase, *global warming*. As always, the collision between standards-approval and politics leaves innocent students as the collateral damage. If we look at the best possible value that the Common Core and NGSS can bring to the classroom, we still face a logistical challenge: the very political cost and logistical training cost of adopting Common Core, even with the best of intentions, is significantly slowing down the uptake of NGSS and beyond, and this means a widening gap between Math/Language Arts and the rest of our educational portfolio for years to come.

Test-based Accountability

How do we authentically improve student learning across the board? This deceptively simple question is frustrating because, time and again, we demonstrate that pouring attention and resources into a specific classroom can do wonders; yet the same techniques, scaled up, fail to achieve sustained success in other classrooms. Test-based accountability is borne from a desire to create an educational mechanism that is, to student learning, what capitalism claims to be for the economy: a self-correcting system that uses reward and failure to bend everyone's behavior in the direction of success.

President Bush, with *No Child Left Behind*, and President Obama, with *Race to the Top*, enacted massive programs with test-based accountability that have much in common. As characterized by author Diane Ravitch, they both offer a left-right strategy that markets well to the political left and the political right simultaneously. For the left: pedagogical programs and standardization that hope to reduce educational gaps between genders, socio-economic groups and geographic regions. For the right: large contracts to curricula vendors, and school choice and accountability metrics that make schools run like businesses. No Child Left Behind (NCLB) in 2001 forced states to compile detailed information on student performance—significantly, by subgroup. For the first time the achievement gaps between races or middle and lower class students became impossible to deny. For instance, low-income students fare two to three grade levels behind middle-income students by the end of middle school, nationally averaged! But NCLB's statistics also spotlighted the outliers, numerically showing specific classrooms and schools where the gaps were nearly nonexistent. The obvious reaction: let's study these success stories and scale them up, reforming all of education in the image of these few successes.

But this approach depends on quantitative metrics for success and presumes that these numbers will be authentic and lasting. Yet there is little real evidence backing these assumptions. Performance indicators are just statistics, and there will always be regions that look good and regions that look bad—it's in the nature of statistics. But the successful numbers can also be transient. The same classroom that looks outstanding one year may be average the next, and so scaling up school reform using numbers that look good, without really understanding why a classroom was successful one particular year, becomes indistinguishable from day-trading stocks by betting on the ones that are outperforming the average for a particular year.

What's more, as accountability becomes built into school funding in terms of rewards and penalties, middle and elementary schools stop paying attention to subjects that are not represented in the formulae: arts, science, history and civics. When New York City implemented reading and math-intensive programs across the city's districts, the result was poor performance in science and social studies. There is no free lunch. During No Child Left Behind, New York City's emphasis on the accountable subjects—math and reading-- hurt science so much that not a single district in NYC was even able to score at the fiftieth percentile nationally in science.

Another problem with the test-based approach to accountability stems from the fact that the tests becomes not only the instrument for measuring knowledge, but also the teaching goal in the classroom. Teaching to the test harms the students because general learning is supplanted by exercises designed specifically to score well on a test; and of course the test was never designed as curriculum. It was simply supposed to sample learning success after the fact. Several examples drawn from Texas and Chicago demonstrate increasing test scores with a continued inability to answer short-answer questions or demonstrate real changes in long-term learning (see Further Reading at the end of this chapter).

Then we have the more nefarious problem of test-based accountability: redefining success. When NCLB insists that schools show quantitative improvements to proficiency on state-run tests, there are two ways to skin the cat: make students more proficient every year on the same tests, or change the definition of proficiency every year to ensure marked improvement. In 2006, New York students needed 41% on a level 1 test to achieve proficiency; by 2009, the proficiency threshold was 17.6%. In 2007, Texas students achieved 85% proficiency in reading in grades 4 and 8 by state definitions; but the National Assessment of Education Programs test measured proficiency at 28%. Texas was not alone; Tennessee said

90% whilst NAEP measured 26%.

The most toxic aspect of this numbers-focused game is the NCLB insistence that every school student must be proficient in reading and math by 2014, with consequences if schools fail to achieve 100%. Even if proficiency and standards were treated as bare minimums, it would be impossible to authentically reach 100% proficiency, ever. And even if we could, it would not be cause for celebration, because we cannot be proud of achieving bare minimums. But to insist on such goals means that teachers will be laser-focused on quantitative metrics and school districts have to adjust their definitions of success to achieve the goal, since financial consequences wait in the wings for those who fail.

The fundamental problem with this approach is an assumption that there are good schools, bad schools, good teachers and bad teachers; and if we simply numerically identify the good ones and close the bad ones, all will be well. Bill Gates famously said, "If the entire U.S., for two years, had top quartile teachers, the entire difference between us and Japan would vanish." This statement demonstrates the fallacy that teachers and classrooms are numerical concepts, and that teachers who are good this year are good next year. Such stability is utter myth in the complex cultural system we call school, and so test-based accountability is as much a mixed bag as any of its ancestral school reform programs.

The most relevant impact school reform has on technology fluency, the subject of this book, is that it creates a pathological patchwork of attention and inattention: teachers care about specific tests, administrators care about specific subjects, most notably language arts and math, and technology fluency, engineering, history and numerous other subject areas lose as a result. From a standards and testing perspective, what can you do to advocate for and choose schools that prepare your children most authentically for the future? That is the subject of the next section.

Synthesis

You will want to understand the role of standards and testing in your school. To begin with, are standards treated as a comprehensive guide for learning or a floor to be checked from time to time to make sure something critical is not left forgotten during curricular planning? A telling approach is to understand just where the curricula comes from: do the teachers use materials from the big national presses, such as Scholastic? If so, how much do they customize the material?

The more teachers customize, the better perspective and local empowerment you sense, the likelier it will be that the teachers are emotionally engaged with the material, and this will parlay into student excitement. If textbooks from national publishers are used heavily in class, take one home and read it. If you find it dry, boring and poorly done, then imagine what your children will think.

To understand how the school views standards, ask about subjects that are simply not covered by today's tests and standards: civics, history, art, engineering, to name a few. How do the teachers design curricula for these subjects and how do they test student knowledge?

Turning to test-based accountability, first learn about the administration's approach: how is teacher performance evaluated? If the administration uses the national tests to rate teacher performance, you have a telling problem. Most agree that evaluating teachers in this way is inaccurate and also toxic: it forces teachers to focus their class time on the test for their own future's sake, and upends the motivations and goals that should be guiding teacher and classroom success.

Now for test-based accountability and students. How do teachers evaluate the students? Can the teachers tell whole stories of individual student learning—ideally across disciplinary boundaries— or are they evaluating students numerically using the very same tests that the state and nation use? How much time is spent on practice tests leading up to the tests? This is time stolen from true learning opportunities in the classroom. If the teachers see good test performance as a side effect of good teaching, which concentrates holistically on the student, then you have enlightened teachers and, likely, an enlightened administration.

Diane Ravitch concludes by pointing out that curriculum and instruction are far more important than choice and accountability. The school reform trope will fail to live up to expectations, reinventing itself every few years, if it continues to believe in across-the-board fixes having to do with metrics and punishment. Your challenge is to navigate school systems in spite of this overemphasis on the quantitative: if you can find teachers and administrators that view standards and test-based accountability in the right way, you have a much better chance of identifying a school where the students will learn lessons that will help them achieve lifelong fluency.

Standards Reading Resources

THE DEATH AND LIFE OF THE GREAT AMERICAN SCHOOL SYSTEM

Diane Ravitch's book tells the story of recent school reform trends, and how Ravitch herself helped forward policies that she has since regretted. The book looks closely at test-based accountability and the shortcomings of this approach, and teaches the reader to look at educational statistics with a critical eye. This is a must-read if you hope to serve on a school board or PTA committee.

HOW CHILDREN SUCCEED

Paul Tough details the work on grit and character embodied by researchers such as Angela Duckworth, and goes on to explain how programs like No Child Left Behind made achievement gaps impossible to ignore by quantifying them publicly. Much of the book dives into success stories such as the KIPP schools; and one leaves with an understanding of how a complex network of excellence, from enthusiastic teachers to risk-taking administration, can create the best possible environment for children to learn and mature.

STANDARDS INITIATIVE WEBSITES

You can browse standards websites, notably there is www.corestandards.org for the Common Core standards, and www.nextgenscience.org for the Next Generation Science Standards. While you can, in both cases, dive down and read the standards, the trip will not be wholly fulfilling. When you read *Use multiplication and division within 100 to solve word problems in situations involving equal groups, arrays, and measurement quantities*, the issue is, how will this standard be realized in a classroom? Explicitly, all by itself? With curricula designed to inspire kids using real-world, authentic challenges? As a by-product of excellent math experiences that don't even try to focus specifically on such a standard? These websites do not guide you to such questions and answers. Only discussions with your kids and their teachers will do that.

4 DIGITAL LEARNING

The main question is not so much how the new technology can help students learn. Rather, it's what will they do with what they learn? Will they use their knowledge to build...or will they use it to destroy? Only real human beings can help them know the difference—regardless of the medium or the technology used for communication. – Fred Rogers, 1996

When I was in high school, the Texas Instruments scientific calculator arrived with fanfare, and electronics in the classroom transformed overnight from novelty instrument to essential tool for math, science and physics classes. The revolution was exciting and disconcerting because the new technology opened avenues for laboratory work, in-class exploration, homework but also new debates and policies regarding just what technology is acceptable to use during exam time.

That was a memorable shift in education; and yet today's digital learning products promise far greater impact on teaching strategies. Where calculators were nothing more than a new tool with a bit role, digital learning today proposes several ways in which computer systems become essential environments for the educational experience, replacing lessons, lectures, tests—even augmenting the in-school social experience.

This tutorial will introduce you to the most important movements underway in digital learning, both regarding their potential advantages and also the ways in which they are promising more than they can deliver. My goal is to provide you with enough background to make informed choices regarding school and home use of digital learning products with your child.

Why Digital Learning?

One basic theory attracts most entrepreneurs and educators to digital learning tools for every learner in the classroom and thereby move the needle on class performance. The hypothesis is that conventional school only works for students who already have just the right study habits, but that the normal classroom totally disengages numerous other types of students, each of whom needs customized attention. The solution, as proposed through digital learning, is to focus strongly on individual student engagement. Create interactive lessons that are competitive, with points and high scores. This will attract game-players. Turn learning into play in order to show that learning can be fun. Create on-line social networks that enable students to find and reinforce like-minded friend networks during learning.

Since every student's interaction with a digital learning system can be recorded and automatically analyzed, this approach also promises individualized customization. We can collect high-resolution data, improving student-by-student tracking but also enabling highly customized experiences designed to match the child's learning speeds and interests. In this ideal case, digital learning turns drudgery into highly engaging and highly customized play that turns on many students who would never have otherwise succeeded. In the below sections, we discuss three major digital learning strategies gaining traction today as ways to rethink student engagement—each hoping to change the relationship between technology, teachers and learning: gamification, digital-tutors and MOOC's.

1 Gamification

I'm often asked if I think there's something about electronic games that is actually bad for children. What I have come to believe is this: The healthiest playthings for young children are those that a child can make conform to him or her own unique fantasies and feelings. By and large, electronic games do just the opposite. They make a child conform to the program inside the machine. – Fred Rogers, 2002

Gamification is a design principle used in both business and education that focuses on the use of rewards to drive motivation. The key insight is that the combination of clear, near-term goals combined with enjoyable rewards provide both minute-by-minute guidance and the positive feedback that motivate a learner during the work of learning. This means the learning must be broken into bite-size steps, and a system of positive feedback should tie into that step-by-step progress. Badges and competition scores are two such reward systems, one building on scout-like accolades; the other tying into student's competitive instincts, video games and sports associations.

Lynn Clark, author of *The Parent App*, notes that today's youth use digital media as sources and sites for the construction of their personal identity, and so perhaps on-line digital games are also conducive to tying schoolwork directly into the student's sense of identity. What's more, implicit rewards can be built into the very act of engaging in positive social on-line interactions, and so the student's engagement with on-line communities of like-minded fellow students can serve as both a direct reward and as valued social status.

As with any new education strategy, there are extremists on all sides of the gamification debate. There is a frequently repeated notion that on-line digital worlds are better than the real world, and that therefore it is a far more desirable place for learning to happen. Jane McGonigal's book is titled, *Reality is Broken*; Barry Chudakov says *by 2020 we will realize that gaming's ready-made metalife is one of the best ways ever devised to see, understand and improve upon reality.* But the notion of on-line superiority misses a key point, that the real world is the only real world we occupy. Its inconsistencies, challenges and hardships are all worthy of our attention because we each need to learn to navigate them. Gamification and on-line learning can help with this, by providing intermediate levels of challenge and by creating safe spaces for learning to first be nurtured.

But there is a danger that we may oversimplify by steering away from learning for learning's sake. One argument is that gamification makes studying fun, and that school ought to be as fun as a computer game. But several authors also write about the confusion of play and labor: is it acceptable for students to come to believe that all work is fun, as gamification business consultants will sometimes propose? Chore Wars is an example often cited by gamification enthusiasts: turn house chores into domestic, point-scoring battles, and even doing the dishes becomes fun. Is that really how we wish to create a personal sense of responsibility in our children regarding home care?

Gamification is certainly not all bad nor all good. We can extract the best characteristics this approach suggests, as summarized well by Andrew Stott and Carman Neustadter at Simon Fraser University: freedom to fail, rapid feedback, progression, storytelling. These are all elements of computer games that make them highly satisfying and that open a game player up to taking risks, emotionally investing and following through—all qualities we wish to see in our students. And yet the very best teachers I know recognize these same qualities as essential in every conventional classroom.

We ought to be inspired by the success of video games at engaging and retaining children's interests. Gamification is indeed a strategy worth investigating to improve student engagement. But the very best elements of on-line gaming are really the same as those of the most successful classrooms. A great teacher and outstanding course do not need to be gamified, nor should students be insulated from the notion that hard work can be personally motivating, inspiring and rewarding, even when it is not fun and when there are few external rewards.

2 Cognitive Tutors

These days more and more children are being exposed to fancier and fancier machinery. Many schools are using computers in their children's daily routines. No matter how helpful they are as tools (and of course they can be very helpful tools), they don't begin to compare in significance to the teacher/child relationship which is human and mutual. A computer can help you learn to spell "HUG," but it can never know the risk or the joy of actually giving or receiving one. – Fred Rogers, 1996

As gamification has gained traction for engaging with students more effectively, so the idea of fully customized educational learning experiences for each student has also become popular in the curriculum development community. *Cognitive tutors* are a vision for creating individualized student experience by pairing a single student with a computer-based teaching system that adapts to the student's knowledge level and abilities, continually varying the specificity, intensity and explanations to match the student's needs.

Cognitive tutors are exciting because, since a piece of software can know through the login process just which student is using the application, it can keep a long-term record of performance, and it can be designed to scaffold learning carefully and differently for each user. So the appeal of cognitive tutors is technical, educational and at the policy level.

For instance: can computers finally enable the U.S. to break out of its curse of underachievement in, say, mathematics? Math involves a progression of new concepts, heavy drilling on each one, and has easily quantifiable ways of assessing student performance. Indeed, cognitive tutors' first major foray into education was in mathematics for these very reasons.

The challenge you face, as with many things, is separating the big talk about the promise of cognitive tutors from the specifics of actual cognitive tutor systems that are being deployed to real school systems. For example, Carnegie Learning creates the Cognitive Tutor math system, which has been adopted by thousands of schools nationally. Their website shares stories of school success—for instance Dundalk Middle School in Maryland adopted Cognitive Tutor and saw assessment scores skyrocket from 49% proficiency in 2002 to 86% proficiency in 2004. But the New York Times, in a 2011 article, *Inflating the Software Report Card*, noted that the advertising does not mention that the rate stayed at 85% in subsequent years, even though Dundalk dropped Cognitive Tutor because of logistical problems with computer lab time.

As we discovered in the Standards tutorial, every assessment statistic is only partially true. When that proficiency score is advertised to go up, it could be changes in how proficiency is defined by the state; it could be changes to teachers, student body, et cetera. Proficiency is still a poor way to evaluate new educational techniques—and this is bad news for those hoping for a quick fix, since even figuring out if a new technique works turns out to be a very hard problem.

RAND has published an in-depth report on their multi-year evaluation of mathematics cognitive tutors on student achievement and attitude across 140 schools: *Effectiveness of Cognitive Tutor Algebra 1 at Scale*, by Pane et al. The authors report that the first year that Cognitive Tutor was implemented yielded either negative or insignificant effects on students in middle school. For high school, the effects in the first year were more negative than positive. What's more, the students with the largest negative effects on Algebra learning (measured by standardized assessment, unfortunately) were the highest-performing students. The table in the study is convincing, with the top 20% of students in classes doing far worse than the prior year, the next 20% less so, and so forth across the board. This result suggests an opportunity cost for introducing such software: as it interrupts conventional teaching practice, so the students benefiting most from conventional teaching are at risk. The study authors believe this result may relate to the effort of implementing new software, because the second-year results recovered, showing improvement in math proficiency. Perhaps it takes two years to implement such a major change in educational strategy, and there will always be a transient penalty. The good news is that, after two years, the students are learning more math, mostly across the board.

However a careful read of the study's survey form results reveals a more troubling result focused on attitudes. This experiment collected not only data on proficiency using knowledge tests; it also gave regular surveys to the students with questions that would reveal changes in attitude, including the role of computers in learning math; interest in math and technology; the utility of math in the future; confidence in technology; usefulness of technology in employment; future school plans; and even personal opinions about the quality of the math course. The study found a significant trend on only one of all these measures of attitudinal shift: the role of computers in learning math.

In other words, there were no significant attitudinal trends bigger than the software itself, whether in triggering an interest in computing, or in nurturing an excitement for math and technology in one's future. This non-result is important because it reinforces the fact that proficiency is just one part of the picture: cognitive tutors will help some students become more proficient through well-tuned practice, but they will not change individual attitudes effectively. They will have their place, but are not a panacea to student demotivation or disengagement.

The take-home lesson is that digital tutoring will be a tool of value, but the hype surrounding this methodology is troubling. If your school district adopts digital tutors based on advertising regarding proficiency score changes, some skepticism is warranted. Furthermore digital tutoring clearly does not replace direct teacher-classroom interactions that, when they are outstanding, provoke a newfound love for a subject. Software cannot replace human contact, and so it is important that, however cognitive tutors are implemented, the school ensures that there is still time and space for attitudinal engagement in the classroom. After all, a core skill our students learn in school is how to interact and collaborate with diverse peoples.

3 On-Line Courses

There are some things children can do with computers in school that help them express their feelings or communicate with others about something that concerns them. But more often than not, computers are instruments for drill and practice. Right answer or wrong answer. Certain things in this world are cut and dry like that. But most are not. And when a student gets a "wrong" answer, shouldn't a caring teacher be listening and trying to understand why? Sometimes it's a child's humanness that allows him or her to see things a new way...a new way that's somewhere between right and wrong. – Fred Rogers, 1996

I think the best way to understand the motivation behind MOOC's is to share a quote by Daphne Koller, co-founder of Coursera: *I can't believe that we spent so much of our students' time shoveling them into auditoria and having them sit there for 75 minutes while somebody lectured at them.* The fundamental attitude here is that lectures in a classroom are a waste of time because they are one-way, impersonal deliveries that ought to be replaced by two-way, dynamic discussions. But then how do courses provide all the information packed into the lectures, if each class period focuses on interaction and activity? Enter Massive Open Online Courses- MOOC's.

These on-line experiences combine aspects of gamification and cognitive tutoring together to create software-based learning that is both one-on-one, student-to-computer, and massively social, like on-line games, with communities of students who are enrolled together and who forge social relationships alongside the exercises.

Just as cognitive tutors drill a single student, constantly measuring the student's performance and adjusting pacing, so MOOC's break lectures up into very short mini-lectures, usually eight to ten minutes each, bookended by interactive exercises to engage the student, wake them up and test their knowledge incrementally. MOOC's can be entirely self-paced, or they can have a 300,000 student enrollment, with timed tests and homework schedules that apply to all students on one shared clock. In either case the students must be engaged enough to use the on-line resources on their own time, and if there is a physical classroom setting, then that flipped classroom is devoted to discussion and exploration rather than rote teaching.

Two basic types of MOOC have evolved over the past few years: non-profit and for-profit. *Khan Academy* and *edX* are the two most successful non-profit players. In September 2013, edX announced a partnership with Google to create MOOC.org, a website to help universities and teachers create their own coursework for anyone anywhere, built on Google tools. In the for-profit space, *Coursera* and *Udacity* are the major players, providing synchronized coursework with official enrollment periods, homework due dates and exams like conventional courses, but all in the on-line format, with very short lectures punctuated by exercises.

Khan Academy in particular has become a valuable asset for children across a broad range, from grade school through high school. Its collection of nearly 4,000 lectures with automatic exercises focuses mostly on math and physics, but is branching out into social sciences. Khan Academy's deep trove of on-line material is particularly useful for supplementary learning at home, and I strongly encourage parents to explore the site with their children to reinforce math lessons at school.

One interesting unknown facing the MOOC community is profit: the for-profit companies are working hard to both perfect their on-line course authoring tools, and to find strategies for actually turning a profit. While they sign up tens of thousands of students for each course, these students are frequently in the developing world and unable to pay tuition; that is the whole reason they turn to the on-line material. One model likely to play out is a paid accreditation path through each course: you can enroll in the MOOC for free material, but to earn a certificate of completion you must pay.

The evaluations of MOOC-based learning are just as scattered as those of cognitive tutoring systems. At San Jose State University, edX deployed a hybrid Circuit and Electronics course that used on-line lectures hand in hand with in-class Q&A. The result was a pass rate that improved from 55% to 91%, quite an exciting achievement. Yet a Columbia study of Washington community-college students found that students perform less well in exclusively on-line courses than in a face-to-face one, with a gap that was even wider among those with lower GPA's and African-Americans—precisely the groups that we wish to boost in order to make education more equitable.

It is clear that non-profit MOOC material has great value as a supplement to in-school experiences. As for the incorporation of MOOC's into the school curriculum, if it is to succeed it must be a hybrid approach, with both on-line lecture material and in-class interaction time. The MOOC does not provide a comprehensive social learning experience, nor does it replace interacting personally with a teacher who really knows you. Social-emotional development, after all, is a critical goal for our children in school. On-line tools will never provide the ideal environment for social-emotional learning.

Take-Home Lessons

Digital learning technologies can provide real value for your child's classroom. But they can also be a distraction for teachers and students, resulting in a net loss in education quality rather than a clear win. I conclude with four themes to help you evaluate your specific circumstance, and to work with your teachers to ensure digital learning is used positively.

1. IGNORE THE BUSINESS HYPE AND FOCUS ON TRACK RECORD.

Do not accept any study results from digital learning purveyors' websites at face value. The problem with such evidence is two-fold: first, the evidence presented to you is cherry-picked, so it will never give you real insight into how effective a new digital learning tool may be. Second, even a well-balanced study is not a real forecast for what will happen in your child's classroom. Learning success is sensitive to many factors, from teachers and specific student populations to school climate issues, that are outside the control of a study. There are countless stories of technologies that work beautifully in one pilot, then are scaled up to a hundred schools only to show little promise. Instead of starting with a company website, turn to real track records—find classrooms where the digital learning tool is already used, ideally in your own school, and connect with teachers who have real-world experience. They will have relevant and valuable insights to share.

2. DOES THE DIGITAL LEARNING TOOL EMPOWER THE TEACHER?

The right digital learning tools enable the teacher to provide more diverse, customized learning experiences to every student. In the best case, teachers are thus more empowered by digital learning because they can collect and study individualized data about each student, then adjust that student's challenges to best fit their needs. But flipping a classroom or studying individual student performance takes significant time out of lesson preparation time. Does the teacher have the time to benefit from the digital tools' feedback, or is time such a tight resource that the teacher has even less freedom to plan great lessons because of time caught up with digital learning bureaucracy? If the digital learning system is rigid, imposing its own schedule upon the classroom or forcing the teacher to reorder lessons to fit the on-line game's concept ordering, then this is a red flag, because the system is disempowering and railroading the teacher rather than providing greater freedom for expressiveness.

3. PARTICIPATION WILL GIVE YOU INSIGHT.

In *The Parent App*, Lynn Clark writes about Parental Mediation—parents taking an active role in managing their children's experiences with digital media. In defining this type of role, Clark encourages direct involvement between parents and their children's media viewing experiences. Two of these strategies will particularly help you develop a strong insight for just how digital tools are being used by your child.

Active mediation: start by talking to your child about digital learning; what are they doing on-line, at home and at school, that supports their class experiences? Which websites are used, and how long do they spend at each?

Coviewing: next, have your child take you on an authentic tour through their digital learning resources. Sit shoulder to shoulder while the student plays the learning game, takes an on-line Khan Academy class, or logs into a cognitive tutor website and works on math skills. Use your observations to learn how your child is treating this on-line time, and whether you feel she is truly learning from the experience.

4. HOW ARE STUDENT ATTITUDES BEING IMPROVED?

In the end, the single most important lesson to keep in mind is that digital learning tools will not shift student attitudes. For the self-directed student who enjoys deep dives to gain new knowledge, digital learning provides wonderful new resources. This effect is much like an excellent public library: for the self-motivated, self-directed student, the library is a place filled with wonder and adventure. But the library, on its own, does not instill a love of learning in the first place—that is the result of long-term, social interaction with parents and teachers. Ensure that all of your child's caregivers are actively instilling a strong, positive attitude towards learning, rather than hoping that gamification, cognitive tutors or flipped classrooms will automatically compensate for poor student motivation.

To change the attitudes of our children, the first step we must take is to change the attitudes of the adults in our childrens' lives. The child is connected to her teachers and to her parents for the duration of the educational experience. When teachers and parents improve their attitudes toward learning, self-empowerment and technology fluency, then the positive vibes uplift our children as well, because attitudes are strongly contagious, and are shaped by the experiences we value in our lives.

But that trust doesn't happen by accident. And there are no short cuts. I'm firmly convinced that it's through relationships that we grow best. And, it's through relationships that we learn best. That's why, from the start, we wanted the Neighborhood to have the atmosphere of a "visit" between me and our television neighbors. – Fred Rogers, 1996

Digital Learning Reading Resources

GAMIFICATION: EXPERTS EXPECT 'GAME LAYERS' TO EXPAND IN THE FUTURE, WITH POSITIVE AND NEGATIVE RESULTS
The Pew Research Center's report on gamification, published in 2012, reviews diverse experts' opinions on how gamification provides positive and negative influences, and how it will be used in education over the next decade.

ANALYSIS OF GAMIFICATION IN EDUCATION
This paper by Andrew Stott and Carman Neustaedter at Simon Fraser University is a very accessible description of three case studies for how gamification has been used in three separate courses to change student experiences. The authors do an outstanding job of explaining the most important elements of gamification that can improve learning, and they conclude by demonstrating that a one-size-fits-all mentality is inappropriate for gamification of classes. Rather, the integration of gaming into teaching requires careful calibration to the specific culture of each classroom.

THE PROFESSORS WHO MAKE THE MOOCS BY STEVE KOLOWICH, THE CHRONICLE OF HIGHER EDUCATION

MOOCS TRANFORM HIGHER EDUCATION AND SCIENCE BY M. MITCHELL WALDROP, NATURE MAGAZINE AND SCIENTIFIC AMERICAN

These two on-line reports describe university professors around the world who are creating on-line MOOC teaching content, provide data regarding the investment of time required by each professor and how course accreditation is likely to evolve with MOOC's ever-growing needs to turn a profit. This is a good pair of readings to understand the politics and velocity of the MOOC movement at the university level.

EFFECTIVENESS OF COGNITIVE TUTOR ALGEBRA I AT SCALE
This long-format report by Pane et al. at RAND evaluates one specific mathematics cognitive tutor across more than 140 middle

and high schools in seven states. The report is extremely deep, providing ample detail regarding study procedures and outcomes, which are mixed, and represents the most comprehensive such analysis.

THE PARENT APP

Lynn Clark's book is a cultural study of how parents and children across varying income levels negotiate the child's use of digital media, including TV, smartphones and the Internet. By cutting across socio-economic divides, Clark paints a picture of diversity and identifies useful strategies for parents to consider in mediating or limiting the consumption of digital media in the home. I highly recommend reading this book.

REALITY IS BROKEN

Jane McGonigal is a foremost champion of gamification as a way of engaging disaffected youth through the digital medium. Without irony, she promotes the on-line world as an improvement over the problems of the physical world, and suggests that games can be designed to help us improve and perfect the real world over time. This hyper-optimistic view of gaming treats digital learning as more social, more engaging and more fun than other forms of learning.

5 FIRST STEPS

Book 1 has been issue-focused, discussing STEM, education policy and digital learning. Book 2 will offer a series of recipes for how you might engage with your child to nurture the skills that develop their technology fluency, and in turn maximize their chance of success in the technology-focused world of our future. But there are first steps that I believe can set you on a path to truly teaming with your child and your child's educators to serve her future. This chapter presents a starting recipe for your consideration, in the form of a four-step plan: Recognition, Attention, Evaluation, Participation.

1. Recognition
Many like to put their hope solidly in the hands of the school. After all, school is supposed to create the education environment that shapes our children's knowledge for the future, so surely school will do the right thing for the technology-heavy future we face. But recall that just 20% of a child's waking hours are spent at school—a small minority of their time. And remember that Silo STEM, test-based accountability and misapplied digital learning tools are all potential wrong turns that could make that 20% time much less effective than you are hoping. What's more, many of the studies I have quoted reach the same, key conclusion regarding a student's chance of success in the school environment: it all depends on attitude, and school is not good at changing an individual student's attitude about

41

learning and technology, not even with the coolest, gamified digital app's.

This brings us to *Recognition*. You need to start by recognizing full well that what you do as a parent matters hugely. You are the one adult with the best means to set up your child for our technology future. The good news is that there are no technology prerequisites for this job; you do not need to be a tech wizard in order to encourage technology fluency in all the right ways. You can learn together with your child, sitting side by side, and in fact this is the very best way to demonstrate the love of learning that will serve her well throughout her life. You do not even need a computer at home—everything I suggest below works using diverse, low-cost resources.

What you will need is <u>time</u>. There are no shortcuts to developing tech fluency, and there is no way to outsource the parent's role to school, after-school or video games. This no shortcuts bit is just like good nutrition: in fact, everyone will market quick fixes to you, from a simple app that teaches your child math to a great little Android tablet that will make her tech-savvy. And just like any processed-food advertisement that supposedly gives you a balanced meal, it's all just empty marketing. With nutrition, the only real solution is to start with balanced, basic ingredients and take the time to care about mealtime. With technology fluency, you can begin with the recognition that you are the most important influence in your child's technology future, and then you invest quality time into building that future out of authentic interactions with your child.

2. Attention

It is so easy to be constantly in a state of distraction, responding to incoming messages on mobile devices, putting out fires at work and amongst our families, forever in the mode of reaction to others' priorities around us. Does operating reflexively like this provide best for our family's future? What seems urgent can cast a cloud over the much more important aspects of life: reading nightly with a child can be canceled repeatedly because, each night, there is an admittedly unique emergency at work that requires attention. Add up all these special cases, and the gentle, long-term relationships that matter most suffer the greatest loss of attention.

Being mindful, always, of this slippery slope of twisted priorities is a very important first step to creating the boundaries and habits of mind that will enable you to give your child, and their developmental and technology environment, the full attention they deserve. Your ability to tune out others' priorities and concentrate on your child-parent relationship will be a powerful gift towards the future because you will become steeped in your child's world. You will be their personal expert, able to bring the most important resource to bear for their future: your caring decisions.

Awareness also extends beyond the relationship you nurture with your child; your understanding of the technology landscape as a whole will give you the power to participate with your child as you explore technology and achieve technology fluency together. As always, the best pathway to awareness is through personal human contact. Look at your social circles and see if you can identify people who can keep you up to date regarding modern technology. Chat with them often. Find a designer, software engineer, architect, businessperson, journalist or photographer and ask them about technology in their career: what's hot, and how is technology changing in ways that are relevant to their work today? These are all highly creative jobs that depend heavily on fast-changing technology, and so the conversations you have with individuals in these fields will be invaluable for helping you stay aware of what technologies will be most relevant to your child.

There are also a great number of printed and on-line written resources that can provide very good background reading. At the end of each tutorial chapter I have listed Reading Resources, and these are good first steps. At the bare minimum, I strongly recommend you start by adding three books to your personal reading list: THE DEATH AND LIFE OF THE GREAT AMERICAN SCHOOL

SYSTEM, HOW CHILDREN SUCCEED, and THE PARENT APP.

The Internet serves several excellent websites that host very good summaries of recent changes in education policy as they happen. I recommend three websites in particular:

blogs.kqed.org/mindshift
Mind/Shift is KQED San Francisco's blog, with posts every few days about technology-rich learning as well as education in-school and out-of-school. The articles are naturally very pro-technology, but with your critical eye in place, the topics are extremely timely.

edutopia.org
Edutopia is an on-line publication of the Lucas Foundation (yes, the same Lucas who created Star Wars) and is devoted to tales of innovation in the formal K-12 schooling system. The articles are published far less frequently than Mind/Shift, but also take a strongly pro-technology stance, featuring cases where digital learning has greatly improved outcomes. The most informed teachers and school administrators pay careful attention to Edutopia's publications, and so this is a good way for you to establish some common ground with them.

dmlhub.net
Macarthur Foundation is the eight hundred pound gorilla in the area of digital learning technology. Their decision to put marketing muscle and investment behind specific education technology programs has major impact on where American technology learning goes. DML (Digital Media and Learning) organizes their vision and features their spending priorities.

In addition to these websites that are devoted to technology-focused education, I perform regular news searches using news.google.com. I enter one of these phrases in the search bar and browse the resulting news items:

```
STEM evaluation            online education
common core assessment     common core standards
teacher accountability     digital learning
```

3. Evaluation

You recognize the importance of your role, and you are attentive to your child and her technology environment. The next step is to go local, observing the tech fluency state of your own child, as well as the technology stance of your local school. If your child is five, they have a technology mindset that is helpful to understand as a starting point.

We can break down this technology mindset into two categories: Power and Relevance. Power is about the perceived power relationship your child has to technology, writ large. Is she empowered by technology already, feeling that devices such as computers and tablets are tools in toolbox, readily applied to any problem? Or does she see fragile, magical black boxes that can only be used one prescribed way, else they may break. Below are ten action statements that exemplify the mentality you are probing. Does your child agree with at least five of these, directly through conversation or indirectly through your observation? If so, she already has an empowered power mindset toward technology. If not, the underlying relationship between your child and technology may need serious reflection.

When a toy is broken, I take it apart out of curiosity.
I tinker with wood, craft materials, saws and glue to make toys.
When I have questions, I search for answers on the Internet.
When I see a bug I don't recognize, I look it up on-line.
When a computer misbehaves, I blame the computer's software rather than myself and work around the problem.
I use a computer to publish (pictures, videos, stories).
When my parents have trouble with settings on their computer, table or phone, I help figure it out for them.
I use on-line digital learning websites such as Khan Academy,

Code Academy, IXL.
I set up my own favorite screen savers on tablets and phones in the house.
When someone in my family has a question, I research it on the Internet for them.

Another enlightening exercise is creating a *Producer/Consumer Table*. Sit with your child and together list all the different ways in which she can use a computer. Once the list is complete, rewrite the list in three columns, labeled left-to-right as *Produce*, *Interact* and *Consume*. Put activities in the *Consume* column if they involve using apps, websites or programs on the computer to consume media: watch a show, read cartoons, look at other people's blogs and galleries. Put activities under *Produce* if they are all about creatively making new media: write poems, write stories, publish a blog, create a picture catalog, modify images, make and edit videos. Finally, you will have many activities that are interactive and engaging, but not completely production-oriented: use interactive message boards, play video games, use Khan Academy, run a touch-typing tutor. Put all these activities under *Interact*. If the activities are evenly distributed between *Produce*, *Consume* and *Interact*, then you are doing very well indeed. If there are nearly no activities under *Produce*, and the *Interact* category lacks creative or knowledge-building examples, then there is room for mindful improvement.

Relevance is the second technology mindset that we can notice, and this is more applicable to older children, certainly 8 years of age and older. The question of relevance stems from the fact that accelerating technologies, both robotics and otherwise, are guaranteeing that no matter what career our child chooses, technology will play a critical role in her success. More bluntly, jobs will be scarce, and those who are employed will be the ones who know how to fluently leverage technology in service of their chosen careers.

Talk with your child about their career interests, and ask her how she thinks computers and software might be relevant. No matter what career she is contemplating, computers will be central to day-to-day actions: a fashion designer will design, simulate and render dresses on-line; a musician will use audio software to remix and publish; a businessperson will create interactive sales and marketing tools. If this is second nature to your child, that is an excellent starting point, for she will understand the relevance of technology fluency to her possible futures. If she sees computers as nothing but social media tools for maintaining friendships, then there is much to learn in creating a sense of the creative possibilities unleashed by bringing personal passion together with bleeding-edge tech innovation.

To understand the technology stance of your school, consider your parent-teacher conferences. The parents and the teacher are colleagues and teammates, working together to create the best possible learning and nurturing environment for each child. This is why it is so powerful and effective to use teacher-parent meetings to ask the teacher what you can be doing at home that supports and extends your child's school experiences. Your authentic questions show the teacher that you care about home-school consistency, that you are ready to devote your time so that, as one team, you can all work together. As you forge a positive, meaningful relationship with your child's teacher, you set yourself up as an engaged, non-confrontational parent who is friendly and willing to learn. You can also use this positive relationship to understand the school's attitudes on the three tutorial topics of this book, because this will help you triage how you can improve conditions.

On the topic of STEM, has the school embraced Silo STEM, treating each discipline in STEM as its own island of expertise and knowledge? A good indicator is to notice whether science and math are coordinated into integrated experiences for the students. How about STEAM—does the school add in creativity via 'A' for art, or are they laser-focused on STEM? Any evidence you find that creativity and art are being infused into STEM is very good news.

If Silo STEM is the name of the game, you need to be well aware of this. Your child may find one or more isolated disciplines to be uninspiring, and you will need to work hard to create out-of-school experiences that are more holistic, even as you push for change at school. One simple example: your child is faced with Silo STEM and finds science completely boring. Find your local parks conservancy group and volunteer your family to help identify invasives and steward the local park. The program will infuse biology and science with a sense of ecological value, and this can be a turning point for a child looking for school lessons to have authentic life relevance.

For Standards and Accountability, it can be very helpful to understand how the teachers are evaluated. If teacher performance equals standardized test score results from the students, then all your alarm bells will go off. The teachers, in spite of their very best nature, will be railroaded into concentrating class time on test-taking rather than genuine learning, and few students prosper under these conditions. If teacher evaluation is done by peer evaluation, classroom observation and more qualitative demonstrations of student learning, then the teacher will have the room to experiment, customize and prosper.

On the topic of Digital Learning, you want to understand the school's technology policy. How and when are computers used at school? Is computer use infused throughout disciplines (very good) or is there a special computer lab period where students "learn to use computers" (very bad). What level of computer use is expected of students outside of school for homework, whether at the library or at home? If assignments never depend on computer research tools, that is an opportunity lost. If homework is, at times, published via on-line tools, then your child will benefit by learning to produce rather than just consume via technology.

Another interesting differentiator between schools is their policy regarding electronics. Some districts ban all mobile devices, even taking away all phones and tablets on entry and returning them to students only after the school bell rings. At the other extreme, districts may allow all mobile devices and publish clear honor guidelines on acceptable use standards. The latter demonstrates that the schools are engaged in teaching good technology usage behavior rather than simply avoiding the subject blindly. Such tech use policies are a great start for the same types of rules you can consider in your own home. One final question about technology pathways merits your curiosity: what support is offered at school for students with a keen interest in technology, such as computer programming, web publishing and related topics? If there are special pathways open for pursuing technology-focused hobbies, you and your child will want to be aware of them early.

4. Participation

You are an engaged, attentive parent, and you have established a productive and positive relationship with your child's teacher. The final step in this basic recipe for tech fluency development is the most time-consuming and rewarding of all: *participation.* To begin, become completely inclusive. In everything technological that you yourself do, include your child whenever possible. Suppose you are struggling to connect a new printer to your laptop. Go through the installation process, the web research and the trial and error with your child alongside, and think out loud about the problem-solving process and your frustration.

Next, practice *co-learning.* Whenever your child is learning something new—for instance beginning to do some math exercises using Khan Academy—sit with them and learn alongside them. If your child is learning to make a simple website on-line, and you have never made a website with raw HTML, then take the opportunity to learn right with your child. Your curiosity and enthusiasm to learn will be contagious, and you will also be establishing common technology education memories that will

49

give you reserves for conversations and future explorations.

Third, give your child the chance to be a *teacher*. When they have discovered how to set the alarm on your mobile, change your background and make the ringer silent using special keystrokes—and they will invariably learn to do all this better than you—then ask them to teach you. Providing your child with the opportunity to teach will build her technological self-confidence and provide her with the pride of passing on knowledge.

Fourth, ensure through personal participation that your child's use of technology weaves *creativity* and technology together. Strongly creative practices bring all parts of her brain into the action equation, and combining creative expression with technology demonstrates that tech and art are not at all exclusive, but rather that they build upon one-another in mutual stimulation. Your goal is to break any stereotypes your child may have about technology being a narrowly applicable, specialized device, good for Facebook and video games and little else. The opportunities for combining creativity and tech are nearly limitless: purchase Adobe Lightroom and have your child photograph, crop and adjust digital photos, and organize the images into viewing galleries. Create an on-line blog when you take a vacation, and have your child take charge of every daily entry, shared with all the extended family.

Finally, make use of the very best on-line, interactive educational tools. My all-time favorite is Khan Academy, and the best segments of this resource are math and coding. These two segments are heavily interactive, rather than being mainly about watching short video segments; and they match skill-development challenges to your child's real-time learning. You can certainly begin using Khan Academy when your child is eight years old, and possibly even younger.

Of course, participation does not simply extend to your parent-child relationship at home. You can also use your parent-teacher time at school as a stepping stone to become an active participant. In terms of your school's tech policy, if you discovered that the policy is based on banning use rather than publishing a considered, responsible honor code, then volunteer to help the school consider rule changes. If you determined that technology is Balkanized into its own class, or taught in the context of Silo STEM, then you can improve the technology experience for your child as well as for all students by making an effort to re-envision school curricula. This is a daunting task and takes great patience, but of course our children make all such efforts well worth the time invested.

Roles

Every member of our child's ecosystem has a critical role to play in her well-being. Let us revisit some of the roles and responsibilities that are essential to our ecosystem's health:

Parents The parents represent half the equation in ensuring home-school consistency, and this consistency is a requirement for students to develop self-confidence, courage and eventually a personal conviction that all problems can be overcome. The single biggest challenge parents face is, of course, time. As a parent, you have no spare time. It is all too easy to provide less than children need because work and life are constantly making demands. Yet there will be no tech fluency without a healthy and vigorous home-school partnership between parents and teachers. Parents: your engagement with school, with teachers, and of course with your child predetermines any chance for strong learning, powerful self-confidence and authentic technology fluency.

Children The child needs to develop a deep love of learning, and this flows directly from the flowering of an inquisitive mind, entertained constantly with questions and curiosities. These

51

lessons cannot start in middle school or even lower school: love of learning comes from the experiences of early childhood years, from birth to 4 years of age. Given love of learning, the child has the opportunity to develop problem-solving skills. With the support of parents and teachers, the child will see that all problems can be overcome with perseverance and effort. Next, the child who has a love of learning and a willingness to overcome problems needs the support to develop creativity. Creativity is, in its essence, problem-solving. When you make a piece of art, you are solving constraints and problems to create something expressive out of limited materials. Thus creativity is forever entangled with the courage and self-directed power to see problems, to engage with them, and to overcome them through passion and intellect. Parents, teachers—you provide the environment in which students develop and grow this core skill. Finally, the child who finds herself in a safe environment also learns the power of experimentation: to try, to recognize error and then to try again. Blocks in pre-kindergarten enable a child to see how putting the small block on the bottom of a tower causes it to be unstable, and the child experiments, recognizes the failure, and changes her strategy in the human cycle that stretches from art practice all the way to the scientific method. Your child's environment must support love of learning, problem-solving, creativity and experimentation from birth forward.

Teacher The teacher is a facilitator on many levels. As a facilitator between technology and the child, the teacher helps observe and understand the child's needs as she develops a connection to technology. The teacher must have complete knowledge about each child, enough to connect on an individual basis, recognizing her individual talents and interests and transforming those underlying sensitivities to learning moments. And all this occurs, not simply between teacher and child, but between teacher, child and parents. In addition, teachers create scaffolded opportunities for exploration. Scaffolds are important stepstools that ensure that children surmount challenges, then use what they have learnt during the next exploration. In short teachers create the environment where learning is possible and where the value of learning is clear.

Administration For technology fluency to have a chance—indeed, for student learning to succeed at all—the philosophy of the administration and the teachers must be aligned. Just as with home-school consistency, it is simply impossible for a teacher to succeed, long-term, without institutional consistency. Teachers needs support, and administrations must empower the very best in teaching practice on a daily basis.

Conclusion

The recipe I present above is certainly just the tip of the iceberg. What truly succeeds for you and your family will be the product of your ingenuity, your specific school and social context and the overall technology fluency that your family enjoys in the first place. There are also many resources that you may find helpful in surveying the techniques you might use to facilitate technology fluency. In the research literature, one particularly apt article is PARENTS AS LEARNING PARTNERS IN THE DEVELOPMENT OF TECHNOLOGICAL FLUENCY by Brigid Barron and collaborators at Stanford University (2009). You can download this and other research articles for free at www.google.com/scholar. I particularly like Table 3, where the authors list seven types of parent roles they witnessed in tech fluency learning at home:

> **Teacher**: the parent teaches the child.
> **Project Collaborator**: the parent and child do a tech project together.
> **Learning Broker**: parent finds and creates new tech learning opportunities for child.
> **Resource Provider**: parent provides physical resources to child.
> **Nontechnical consultant**: parent provides encouragement and advice to child as child forges into tech spaces.
> **Employer**: child provides technical services to parent.
> **Learner**: child teaches parent.

For me, the most exciting roles in the list above—*employer* and *learner*—are powerful because your child is the expert, and you are the beneficiary of their knowledge. Giving your child a new role as teacher and knowledge provider reinforces that she can study, learn and provide caring, positive impact thanks to the knowledge she has acquired. This is the very best sort of feedback, and all it requires is for parents to express their needs, ask children for genuine help, and celebrate the new child-parent relationship that results. Technology is fast-changing, and it is quite appropriate for the youngest generation to be the wisest generation in understanding the new and helping us all make sense of the unfamiliar.

By being mindful of technology in the home and at school, and by actively working to be aware of recent trends in technology futures and in education technology, you will set your child up to have the best possible chance at a tech fluent future. In a time of great economic uncertainty and social upheaval, thanks to massive income inequality and robot-triggered underemployment, that tech fluency is the best insurance policy to ensure that your child will not be a victim of technology, but rather an innovator who helps reinvent the future of technology for a better world.

ABOUT THE AUTHOR

Illah R. Nourbakhsh is Professor of Robotics, director of the Community Robotics, Education and Technology Empowerment (CREATE) lab and head of the Robotics Masters Program in The Robotics Institute at Carnegie Mellon University. His current research projects explore community-based robotics, including educational and social robotics and ways to use robotic technology to empower individuals and communities. The CREATE Lab's researchers lead diverse projects, from the application of GigaPan technology to scientific, citizen science and educational endeavours internationally; Hear Me, a project that uses technology to empower students to become leads in advocating for meaningful social change; Arts and Bots, a program for creative art and robotics fusion in middle school; Message from Me, a new system of communication between pre-K children and their parents to improve home-school consistency; BodyTrack, an empowerment program that enables citizens to capture personal health; Speck (www.specksensor.com), a device empowering communities to measure and improve their air quality; and many other such projects.. The CREATE Lab's programs have already engaged more than 23,000 people globally, and the CREATE Satellite program is forging additional CREATE lab partners in new geographic zones. While on leave from Carnegie Mellon in 2004, Illah served as Robotics Group lead at NASA/Ames Research Center. He earned his bachelor's, master's and PhD in computer science at Stanford University and has been a faculty member of Carnegie Mellon since 1997. In 2009, the National Academy of Sciences named him a Kavli Fellow. In 2013 he was inducted into the June Harless West Virginia Hall of Fame. He is co-author of the MIT Press textbook, INTRODUCTION TO AUTONOMOUS MOBILE ROBOTS and author of the MIT Press book , ROBOT FUTURES.

Made in the USA
Middletown, DE
04 May 2015